The Apostles Gospel

Paul Pavao

The Apostles' Gospel
By Paul Pavao

Published by:
    Greatest Stories Ever Told
    P.O. Box 307
    Selmer, TN 38375

admin@christian-history.org
www.christian-history.org

ISBN, print ed.: 978-0-9888119-3-5

Copyright © 2013 by Paul Pavao

All rights reserved. No part of this book may be reproduced or transmitted in any form or by any means, electronic or mechanical, including photocopying, recording, or by any information storage and retrieval system, without written permission from the author or publisher, except for the inclusion of brief quotations in a review.

Cover art by Esther Pavao. Copyright © 2013. All rights reserved.

All Scripture references are from the World English Bible (WEB) and are in the public domain.

Preface

I had a deadly form of leukemia. Now I don't. I have a second chance at life, and I want to make it count.

God formed me to love the truth, and he gave me a compulsion to pursue it that's stronger than sleep, hunger, or fear of embarrassment or rejection. As a result, my obsession with the truth has been remarkably painful.

Truth is more than what is found in books. Jesus Christ is the Truth, and it is only those who follow him in Spirit who can also follow him in truth.

No human mind can be trusted to discover the truth on its own. Every subject I write about has been set carefully upon and tested by what the Scriptures call "the pillar and foundation of the truth": the church (1 Tim. 3:15). Though I confront and transgress custom—the traditions of men—all the time, I dare not ever defy the church.

What I mean by that can best be explained by reading what I write. The pursuit of the truth is not simple.

I am a historian. I am an amateur, but a very experienced and very honest one, with considerable qualifications as a student. Not the least of those qualifications is my submission to and approval by the saints wherever they are gathered.

I believe the teachings that mattered to the apostles can be known both from Scripture and from history if we who are called to teach and lead the flock of God will pursue the truth, and not our own gain, together.

Dedication

To God, our Father, who made me to love what's true, drew me with infinite love, and forced me to be honest.

To our Lord, Jesus Christ, who is the Truth and our model for courage and honesty.

To the Holy Spirit, without whom, despite all my good intentions, I would accomplish no good.

To Christ's church in Selmer and its many friends: Thank you for honoring the truth even when custom demanded you avoid it.

To my wife, Lorie, my faithful companion: Your friendship has made this difficult journey a joy. On top of all the strength your support and respect provides, without you I would not be alive to write this book.

To my daughter-in-law, Esther: Without your hard work this book would be just one more unfulfilled wish.

To Alaina: Your commendations, embarrassing as they can be, keep me believing I can do anything in Christ.

To the doctors at Vanderbilt: Thanks for saving my life.

To the nurses at Vanderbilt: Thanks for making it fun.

To my children, whether in the flesh, by marriage, or by shared experience: I watch you when I wonder why I'm still here. My life is for you.

The Gospel of the Apostles

> *"I was not disobedient to the heavenly vision, but declared first to them of Damascus, at Jerusalem, and throughout all the country of Judea, and also to the Gentiles, that they should repent and turn to God, doing works worthy of repentance."* (Acts 26:19-20)

The Gospel is a simple thing, but it does not consist of merely learning a couple theological truths, nor of memorizing a few words that constitute a password into heaven.

There are many who have become convinced that if they understand the atonement—that Jesus died for our sins—then they are saved and have a guaranteed passage into heaven. Still others are convinced that if they remember to plead the blood of Jesus at the gates of heaven, where they think they will appear immediately after they die, then those gates will swing open to give them "entrance into the eternal kingdom of our Lord and Savior, Jesus Christ" (2 Pet. 1:11).

Many years ago, my wife and I joined an evangelism program called *Continuing Witness Training*. My wife was on a team that had just asked a man, "If you died tonight, do you know for certain you would go to heaven?"

He replied, "Oh, yes. I trust in the blood of Jesus."

The team then turned their attention to others in the home. Later, my wife overheard the first man saying to someone else in the household, "The next time, just tell them 'the blood of Jesus' or 'I believe in Jesus.' They move on to other people every time."

This sort of preaching is typical of evangelicals. In fact, *The Christian Writer's Manual of Style*, an official reference for Zondervan, *defines* evangelical, among other criteria, as believing in "salvation by faith in the atoning death of Christ."[1]

No one can plausibly deny that the apostles taught the atoning death of Christ as a central tenet of Christianity; indeed, as the center of the history of the universe.

But is it the Gospel they preached to the lost?

Paul explained the Gospel[2] that he preached in the quote that opens up this chapter. He declared to them of Damascus, of Jerusalem, throughout all the country of

---

[1] Robert Hudson, ed.; "Evangelical"; *The Christian Writers Style of Manual* [Zondervan: Grand Rapids,MI; 2004]; "Evangelical")

[2] The word Gospel means "good tidings" or "good news." The verb form, *euangelizo*, means "to preach" or "to proclaim good news." In Acts 26:20, Paul used a more general but similar verb, *apangello*, which means to "bring tidings," but does not necessarily denote good tidings. When Paul said he brought tidings or "declared" to the Gentiles the necessity of repentance, he was preaching, and everything Paul preached was the Gospel (Rom. 1:1).

Judea, and also to the Gentiles, that they should repent and turn to God, doing works worthy of repentance.

To Paul, the Gospel was more than memorizing some theology or reciting the right words at the gates of the kingdom of heaven.

It is true enough that Acts 26:20 is incomplete. "Repent and turn to God" is not the only thing Paul said to the lost. Nonetheless, is it not a problem that "repent and turn to God, doing works worthy of repentance" doesn't fit into our Gospel at all? I have been in or interacted with evangelical[3] churches all my adult life. We would never tell the lost to "do works worthy of repentance" in order to be saved. In most churches I've attended, such a teaching would be heresy.

The apostles, however, regularly tell the lost they must repent. The very first time the Gospel was preached, in Jerusalem on the day of Pentecost, those who heard the Gospel cried out, "What shall we do?"

Peter answered them, "Repent, and be baptized, every one of you, in the name of Jesus Christ for the forgiveness of sins, and you will receive the gift of the Holy Spirit" (Acts 2:37-38).

Later, Peter and the brothers from Jerusalem summarized the Gospel with the word "repentance," just as

---

[3] "The term *evangelical* ... can generally be used to mean those Protestants since the Reformation, and especially since the time of John Wesley, who stress the importance of (1) the four gospels, (2) the inerrancy of the Bible, (3) personal conversion, and (4) salvation by faith in the atoning death of Christ. Their worship tends to focus on preaching rather than ritual, and they emphasize each believer's responsibility in evangelism" (*ibid.*)

Paul did. After Peter had preached the Gospel to the Gentile Cornelius, the Jewish brothers in Jerusalem were offended. When he returned from Caesarea, they did not rejoice that the Gospel had gone to the Gentiles. Instead, they accused Peter: "You went into the house of uncircumcised men, and ate with them!" (Acts 11:3).

Fortunately, these brothers were not as stuck in their own ways and opinions as many of us are. Peter explained to them what had happened and won over his Jewish brothers. (Peter based his argument completely on his experience without any reference to Scripture—vv. 4-17—but that is a subject for a different book.) Their conclusion is worth paying attention to:

> "Then God has also granted to the Gentiles repentance to life!" (Acts 11:18)

Think about this. Peter did not correct these Jewish Christians. They are describing the Gospel in general, as it was preached to Cornelius the Gentile and as it was preached to the Jews themselves. They refer to it as "repentance to life."

Is that how you summarize the Gospel?

This is shocking by modern standards, but it is not shocking by apostolic standards. Paul has already summed up his Gospel for us in very similar terms: "I ... declared ... repent and turn to God, doing works worthy of repentance."

The Book of Acts

vs.

The Apostolic Letters

Today we are in the habit of constructing our Gospel from the letters of the apostles. One very well-known presentation of the Gospel is called "the Romans road." The "Gospel" is presented primarily from just three passages:

1. Romans 3:11-23: We're all sinners and fall short of the glory of God.
2. Romans 6:23: Jesus gives us a free gift of eternal life.
3. Romans 10:9-13: We must believe and confess Jesus as Lord to receive the gift.[4]

The problem is not that such an outline is wrong. It is not wrong. We are all sinners, and we have all fallen short of the glory of God. The gift of God really is eternal life, and it is true that we believe, resulting in righteousness, and confess Jesus as Lord, resulting in salvation.

---

[4] cf. Fairchild, Mary, "What is Romans Road"; About.com: http://christianity.about.com/od/conversion/qt/romansroad.htm (accessed April 11, 2013)

The problem is that this is soteriology (the doctrine of salvation) as the apostles outlined it to *Christians*, not the Gospel they preached to *the lost*.

The apostolic letters are written to churches or to scattered groups of Christians. Only Acts records the Gospel the apostles preached to the lost.

There are things that are important for Christians to understand about the salvation. Such knowledge inspires, encourages, convicts, and strengthens us.

The very same bits of knowledge can be worse than useless for the lost, who can be deceived into thinking that they are Christians despite the fact that they have never repented, never died to themselves, and never devoted themselves to "works worthy of repentance."

Why? And What About Faith Only?

We have a very strange idea of what faith is. People say, "I believe in Jesus," but when they run across a verse like, say, Luke 14:33, suddenly they don't seem much like believers at all. There Jesus said:

> "Whoever of you who doesn't renounce all that he has, he can't be my disciple." (Luke 14:33)

It amazes me how many believers do not believe this statement by Jesus. Over and over, I have heard Christians explain why this statement is too extreme to follow. I have had several Christians—really, several—tell me that the fact I am wearing clothes proves that even I don't follow this command by Jesus.

Should it matter to a "believer" whether I follow this verse or not? I did not become the person who issued the command just because I read or quoted the command. Jesus issued the command, and if I am a believer in Jesus, should I not want to know what he meant by the command so that I can follow it? Am I really a believer in Jesus if I consider any of his commands too extreme to follow?

It does not take an excursion into ancient Greek to figure out that someone who claims to believe in a religion or a person, but who disagrees with that religion or person, is not really a believer. Even in English, believing means believing. If you believe in Jesus, then you believe the things he teaches.

Years ago, my wife and I were in a Sunday school class with three other couples. We were reading Matthew 6 together, and we got to the part where Jesus said, "If you don't forgive men their trespasses, neither will your Father forgive your trespasses" (v. 15).

The Bible study leader's exposition of this verse was unforgettable: "That's not true, of course," he said.

My wife and I both reacted with shock. *What did he say?*

He went on to explain that we are forgiven already because Jesus died for our sins and we had believed in him. It doesn't matter what we do now, he explained, because we are not saved by works but by faith.

We weren't interested in his theology. It would have been different if he had been explaining what Jesus meant. Instead, he was explaining why *Jesus was wrong*.

No one took our side. All three couples took a stand against us. "It doesn't matter whether we forgive or don't forgive. All our sins are forgiven by the blood of Jesus."

These people felt like all their sins—past, present, and future—were forgiven because of their faith in Jesus, *even if Jesus said they weren't.*

Is it not clear that by disbelieving Jesus, they are establishing that they have no faith in Jesus?

They do have faith in the theology taught to them by their church; however, when it came down to a conflict between their church's theology and Jesus, they chose their church's theology.

The apostles knew of no such faith. Jesus had given them a commission: to preach the Gospel to the entire world. That commission had one very important stipulation in it:

> "Go and make disciples of all nations, baptizing them in the name of the Father and of the Son and of the Holy Spirit, *teaching them to observe all things that I have commanded you.*" (Matt. 28:19-20, emphasis mine)

This is the faith that the apostles knew. It involved observing everything that Jesus commanded. It was a faith in Jesus, not in some theological truths about Jesus.

Faith in Jesus vs. Faith in Facts

We evangelicals love knowledge. We love to defend our doctrines. We love knowledge so much that we have turned our faith away from Jesus and directed it toward facts about Jesus.

We teach people to believe that Jesus died for their sins. We teach people to believe that heaven is a free gift. We teach people to believe that salvation is apart from works.

We are failing, however, to teach them to believe in Jesus, the one Being in the universe who can really save them.

The Sunday school class I described earlier is evidence of that. Those three couples, however, are not the only ones I have met who call themselves followers of Christ but don't believe the things he said.

As a young Christian, a singles group leader asked me to lead a five-minute devotion at one of our meetings. I was given no time to prepare, and the leader explained she was confident I could come up with something.

I chose Matthew 5:38-40 because I had already been thinking about Jesus' statement, "Don't resist him who is evil." I talked about turning the other cheek and going the extra mile, which are mentioned in that passage as well.

When I was done, the leader told me, "That was really good, but you need to remember that Jesus was being extreme in that passage. We don't want to be too radical."

I am not denying that some of these "hard sayings of Jesus" are subject to interpretation. It would be far better, for example, to throw yourself before your friends in repentance, begging both them and God for help in deliverance from your sin, than to actually cut off your hand or pluck out your eye as Jesus prescribes in Matthew 5:29-30. I agree that Jesus is trying to show us the extremity of sin and the importance of avoiding hell, not calling us to sever body parts.

I agree even that there may be exceptions to resisting an evil man. It is very hard for me to conceive of faulting Sgt. York, the famous World War II conscientious objector who saw his platoon being slaughtered by machine gun fire, for throwing aside his commitment as a conscientious objector, grabbing a gun, and capturing over 100 German soldiers, almost single-handedly.[5]

But we're not talking about interpretations and exceptions here. We're talking about people who have developed a theology that they trust so much that they openly disagree with Jesus and the things he taught. Such are not believers. At least, they are not believers in Jesus, despite their belief in Christian theology.

---

[5] "Sergeant York" is a major motion picture from 1941, starring Gary Cooper. A more accurate version of his story can be found at http://www.sgtyork.org (accessed April 11, 2013).

The Book of Acts
and
the Gospel of the Apostles

There is much more that could be said on the subject of true faith and on the subject of faith and works. Our obsession with theology over Christ has led to a very poor understanding of faith, justification, grace, and even how to get to heaven. I have already written much on those subjects, however.[6] This booklet is to cover the Gospel as preached by the apostles.

If the things written in this booklet are new to you, and you are willing to consider the possibility that they are true, then I ask you to read the entire book of Acts and find out if what I am saying is true. After all, if a disciple is expected to love Jesus more than father or mother (Matt. 10:37) and to forsake all his possessions (Luke 14:33), then surely he can be asked to read Acts, an approximately 25-page booklet, in order to understand his Master's Gospel.

I want to give you a head start by locating each and every apostolic sermon in the Book of Acts and briefly addressing the central point of each. Fortunately, the apostles have made it even easier on us by occasionally summarizing the central points of the Gospel proclamation themselves.

---

[6] See http://www.christian-history.org/doctrine.html

The rest of this booklet will be easier to read if you have the Book of Acts open near you for quick reference.

Acts 2:14-39

This sermon by Peter introduces the New Covenant.[7] Under the New Covenant, every follower of Jesus can receive the Holy Spirit (v. 17).[8] The central point of Peter's sermon is that Jesus, who was killed by the Jews in Jerusalem, was the Christ. God raised him from the dead to prove that he is both Christ and Lord (vv. 32-36).

> "Christ" is a transliteration of the Greek *christos*, which means "one who is anointed." The Hebrew "Messiah" means the same thing. Under the Old Covenant kings, priest and prophets were anointed for their positions. Jesus is our King, High Priest, and *the* Prophet (Acts 3:22; Num. 12:6-8). The idea of the words "Christ" and "Messiah" is that Jesus is the anointed King of God's people.

---

[7] New Covenant is interchangeable in meaning with New Testament. A covenant is an agreement between two parties. The Old Covenant or Old Testament is the agreement between God and Israel. While that covenant was still in force, Jeremiah prophesied of a new covenant between God and Israel, because Israel broke the first one (Jer. 31:31-32). This prophecy was fulfilled when Jesus died, rose again, and gave the Holy Spirit to his apostles so they could go "to the uttermost parts of the earth" (Acts 1:8). He told the Pharisees, "The Kingdom of God will be taken away from you and given to a nation bringing forth its fruit." That holy nation is the Church, born at Pentecost as described in Acts 2.

[8] Cf. Jer. 31:31-34, where the "new covenant" involves "they shall all know me." Also, Ezek. 36:24,27: "I will take you from among the heathen, and gather you out of all countries ... and I will put my spirit within you, and cause you to walk in my statutes, and you will keep my judgments, and do them."

This cut the Jews to the heart, and they cried out, asking what they needed to do.

Peter brought them right back to the center of the New Covenant, which was receiving the Holy Spirit. "Repent, and be baptized, every one of you, in the name of Jesus Christ for the forgiveness of sins, and you will receive the gift of the Holy Spirit" (v. 38).

We can outline his sermon like this:

- What you see is the outpouring of the Holy Spirit upon "all flesh" as promised by the prophet Joel. (vv. 15-17)
- Jesus was approved by God to you by his mighty works. (v. 23)
- You crucified and killed him. (v. 32)
- God raised him from the dead because it was impossible that death should hold him. (v. 24)
- Scriptural references that the Messiah would rise from the dead. (vv. 25-31)
- We apostles are witnesses that he rose from the dead. (v. 32)
- God has proven by the resurrection that Jesus is both Lord and Christ. (v. 36)

The topics covered in our modern Roman's Road Gospel are not covered here. No one is told they are sinners or that they cannot save themselves. Heaven is not even mentioned, nor are any free gifts. Jesus' death is mentioned, but no purpose is assigned to it other than as preparation for the resurrection (vv. 23-24). As we shall see, it is the resurrection, not the crucifixion that is the focus of the apostolic Gospel.

I think it is important to remind us again that there is a difference between the important, encouraging, and edifying theology of salvation that the apostles taught in the letters to the churches and the Gospel that they preached to the lost in Acts.

Acts 3:12-26

This sermon is almost a mirror of Acts 2. Peter accuses the Jews of killing the Prince of Life (v. 15), and then tells them that God raised him from the dead. He then tells them, "Repent therefore, and turn again, that your sins may be blotted out" (v. 19).

Peter expounds on this a little by explaining that Jesus is the Prophet that Moses foretold would come, and he warns, as Moses did, that anyone who did not listen to this Prophet would be destroyed from among the people (vv. 22-23).

Acts 4:8-12

This is a brief defense given to the Pharisees. Once again, the central point is that the Jews crucified Jesus,[9] but God raised him from the dead.

---

[9] The emphasis on the Jews as the ones who killed Jesus is because they were Peter's audience. Over the next few centuries, the Church would soon became embarrassingly anti-Semitic, but Peter was not prejudiced against Jews. He was one!

There is no call to repentance in this sermon because this is not really a sermon. It is a defense of their actions in court: "If we are examined today concerning a good deed done to a crippled man ..." (v. 9).

Acts 4:33

This verse, too, is not a Gospel sermon. It is, however, a summation by Luke (the writer of the Book of Acts) of the Gospel as preached by the apostles. "With great power, the apostles gave their testimony of the resurrection of the Lord Jesus."

Peter has already told us twice that testifying to the resurrection of Christ was the job of the apostles (Acts 2:32 & 3:15). When the apostles chose a successor to Judas Iscariot, who killed himself, they were choosing someone to "become a witness with us of the resurrection" (1:22).

I included this verse to drive home the point that the apostles did not emphasize the atonement, accomplished by the death of Jesus ... at least not to the lost. They saved that emphasis for letters to the churches. To the lost, their job was to proclaim the resurrection of Jesus, which proved him to be the One that God had ordained as Lord and Christ.

> "Let all the house of Israel therefore know certainly that God has made him both Lord and Christ, this Jesus whom you crucified." (2:36)

The goal of the apostles in preaching the Gospel was to bring people into faith in Jesus Christ. The emphasis was on the *person* of Christ, not on the *atonement* of Christ. The atonement would be taught later. For now, the Gospel was that Christ is the Lord who would one day judge the entire world. Therefore, they declared, those who hear the Gospel should repent and believe, submitting themselves to him.

Acts 5:29-33

This is another defense before the Sanhedrin, not an actual Gospel proclamation. Still, it has all the same components as a more typical Gospel sermon. This one is short enough to simply quote. It is, in and of itself, a summation of the apostolic Gospel:

> The God of our Fathers raised up Jesus, whom you killed, hanging him on a tree. God exalted him with his right hand to be a Prince and Savior, to give repentance to Israel, and remission of sins. We are his witnesses of these things; and so also is the Holy Spirit, whom God has given to those who obey him. (vv. 30-32)

This passage could serve as an outline of Peter's sermon in Acts 2. It has exactly the same components:

- You killed Jesus. (v. 30)
- God raised up Jesus. (v. 30)
- We are witnesses of this resurrection. (v. 32)
- The resurrection proves that Jesus is Lord (or Savior, Prince, Christ, or Judge). (v. 31)
- Those who hear should repent. (v. 31)

- Repentance will bring forgiveness of sins and the Holy Spirit. (vv. 31-32)

The only difference is the reaction. In Acts 2, three thousand common Jews—Jews who were not leaders, not members of the Sanhedrin—repented and were baptized. Here in Acts 5, the Jewish leaders react much differently, "But they, when they heard this, were cut to the heart, *and were determined to kill them*" (v. 33, emphasis added).

Let's be careful here not to find an "essential outline" of the Gospel. I am simply listing components that are common to all the Gospel sermons in the Book of Acts. There is flexibility in the points emphasized, in the wording used, and in the exact response called for by the apostles.

These components comprise a story that is repeated over and over as "the Gospel." The more time that was available to the speaker (or writer), the more details that were given.

That is why the four Gospels are called Gospels. They cover the same story, but since there is more time, there are more details. You'll find, however, as you read through the Gospels that they really are Gospels. They emphasize all the same components that are emphasized in the sermons in Acts.

In fact, it is worth noting the conclusion to John's Gospel:

> These [things] are written, that you may believe that Jesus is the Christ, the Son of God, and that believing, you may have life in his name. (20:31)

I don't think we are used to thinking of the "Gospels" as really being the Gospel, but they are. Further, the proclamations of the Gospel given by the apostles to the lost are simply shorter repetitions of those Gospels combined with a call to action: "Repent."

Acts 7:2-53

This sermon by Stephen is powerful, and it can rightly be called a sermon. Primarily, though, it is Stephen's defense before the Sanhedrin. There is no call to action. He does accuse them of killing "the Just One" (v. 52) and of resisting the Holy Spirit just as their fathers did (v. 51).

Acts 8

In Acts 8 there is a lot of discussion concerning the preaching of the Gospel, but no real details to work with. We do know that Philip's preaching resulted in his hearers being baptized (vv. 12-13, 36), but there is really nothing else in the way of details.

Acts 9

In Acts 9, we read of the conversion of Paul, and we read that he preached Christ in the synagogues in Damascus. Again we are given no details other than that Paul preached that Jesus is the Son of God and the Christ.

Acts 10:34-43

This sermon begins with the stunning statement that God accepts those of every nation that fear him and practice righteousness (vv. 34-35). This is not what we are typically taught in Evangelical churches. It is certainly not what I was taught, anyway. We debate whether those who have not heard the Gospel can be saved. Peter tells us they can. God, he says, accepts all those who fear him and practice righteousness.

This can cause us to have to do some difficult theological work aligning Peter's statement with other things we read in the apostles' writings. For example, Jesus said, "I am the way, the truth, and the life. No one comes to the Father, except through me" (Jn. 14:6). For many modern believers, that means people like Cornelius should not be able to be accepted by God.

Rather than be among those that simply reject or ignore what Peter says—which seems to me to be our typical reaction to this little theological conundrum—wouldn't it be preferable to do the difficult theological work?

Paul, too, tells us that it is possible for those that have not heard the Gospel to know who God is and to be justified by him (Rom. 1:20-2:16, esp. 2:14-15). Such a subject is too broad to cover here, and it is unlikely that any of us could reconcile these passages well enough to unite the opinions of all Christians. Nonetheless, our solution cannot be to reject or disagree with Peter, any more than we should reject or disagree with Jesus. Peter was an apostle sent by God to preach the Gospel to us! (Jn. 16:13).

Somehow and some way, God accepts all those who fear him and practice righteousness, even if, like Cornelius, they have not yet heard the Gospel of Jesus.

The rest of Peter's sermon to Cornelius is exactly like the other sermons.

- The Jews killed Jesus. (v. 39)
- God raised him up. (v. 40)
- The apostles were witnesses of this resurrection. (v. 41)
- The resurrection proves that Jesus was ordained by God to judge the living and the dead. (v. 42)
- As a result, through his name everyone who believes in him can receive forgiveness of sins. (v. 43)

Repentance is not specifically mentioned here, but we have seen in previous pages that repentance is not just part, but central to believing in Jesus. The Jewish Christians in Jerusalem, after hearing the story from Peter, concluded that the Gentiles did repent. "Then God," they said, "has also granted to the Gentiles repentance to life" (11:18).

Acts 13:16-41

Here we find Paul's first Gospel sermon in the Scriptures. Once again, it has all the same details:

- The Jews killed Jesus. (vv. 28-29)
- God raised him from the dead. (v. 30)
- The apostles are witnesses of this. (v. 31)
- The resurrection proves that he is the Son of God. (v. 33)

- All who believe in him can be forgiven of sins and justified. (vv. 38-39)

As an aside, let me mention that Paul refers to the other apostles as witnesses of the resurrection, not himself. Paul was not one of the twelve, and he was not a witness of the resurrection, even though he saw and conversed with our resurrected Lord. He says, "He was seen for many days by those who came up with him from Galilee to Jerusalem, who are his witnesses to the people" (v. 31).

Acts 13:48

This verse tells us that it is those who were "appointed" to eternal life who believed. There is much to be said about a verse like this, but it has nothing to do with this booklet. This booklet concerns the proclamation of the Gospel to the lost by the apostles. Just as no apostolic Gospel proclamation includes a discussion of the atonement, so none include a discussion of predetermination either.

Foreknowledge and predestination are interesting subjects, but they are subjects for *Christians*, not the lost. The lost need to be told what Peter told them, which is that the Gospel is "to you, and to your children, and to all who are far off, even as many as the Lord our God will call himself."

Acts 14:14-16

Here, Paul does not preach the Gospel, but he does sum up what he has preached. Paul's summation is that he had taught them "to turn from these vain things to the living God" (v. 15).

Acts 15:13-21

This is the decision of the council at Jerusalem concerning whether or not circumcision and the keeping of the Law of Moses should be added to Paul's Gospel to the Gentiles. The answer given is no. Nothing is said that affects our summation of the apostolic Gospel.

In verse 11, Peter does tell us that those who believe are saved by grace alone, but this does not in any way contradict the Gospel of repentance preached by Jesus and the apostles. Titus 2:11-12, in so many words, tells us that grace teaches us to repent:

> The grace of God has appeared, bringing salvation to all men, instructing us to the intent that, denying ungodliness and worldly lusts, we would live soberly, righteously, and godly in this present world.

Far from contradicting repentance, grace teaches us what repentance is and produces it within us (cf. Rom. 6:14; Eph. 2:8-10). We tend to contrast them, but the apostles did not. In fact, even the churches of the apostles did not. Interestingly enough, we are in possession of a letter from the church of Rome to the church of Corinth which dates from the end of the first century. In it, the author, Clement of Rome, also links grace and repentance:

> Let us look steadfastly to the blood of Christ and see how precious that blood is to God, which, having been shed for our salvation, has set **the grace of**

repentance before the whole world. Let us turn to every age that has passed and learn that ... **the Lord has granted a place of repentance to all those who would be converted to him.**[10]

To the churches that actually heard the apostles and were raised up by them, grace did not conflict with repentance; it produced repentance.

Acts 16:30-33

This is a well-known Gospel passage, cited often by those who would reduce the Gospel to belief in the atonement rather than belief in Christ.

We are told nothing here about the Gospel Paul preached to the Philippian jailer except that it began with "Believe in the Lord Jesus Christ, and you will be saved, you and your household." (v. 31). The passage goes on to tell us that Paul told the jailer and his family much more before they were baptized in the middle of the night (v. 33).

We learn more about baptism in this passage than we do about the apostolic Gospel. Paul baptized the jailer and his family between midnight (v. 25) and the morning (v. 35). Baptism could not have been a "public testimony" in Paul's eyes because there could not have been a public present to be testified to. There were other believers in Philippi (v. 40). If public testimony was the purpose of baptism, Paul could simply have waited and allowed the

---

[10] *First Clement* 7; see http://www.ccel.org/ccel/schaff/anf01.toc.html, accessed Feb. 5, 2013; emphasis mine

jailer and his family to be baptized by the church at a more opportune time. Is this not what we would do today?

As for the Gospel, the very point we are making is that Paul's Gospel, and Peter's, is a call to believe in the Lord Jesus Christ. Notice that Paul did not say, "Believe that Jesus died for your sins, and you will be saved." Such a statement would indeed negate everything I am saying in this booklet. Paul did not say that, however. He said, "Believe in the Lord Jesus Christ, and you will be saved."

Acts 17:22-31

This is a very interesting Gospel sermon by Paul. As far as we know, this is the only Gospel proclamation in our possession that is from an apostle to people that were not familiar with Moses and the Jewish Scriptures.

Nonetheless, except for the introduction that drew from the Athenians' own religion, the Gospel sermon is much like every other. God is commanding all men everywhere to repent (v. 30) because he is going to judge everyone through Jesus Christ (v. 31). He has proven this by raising Jesus from the dead (v. 31).

Acts 19:2-6

Not much is told to us here, either. Paul runs across disciples of John who knew John's Gospel of repentance.

Paul tells them that John preached that people should believe in the one who is to come, who is Jesus. These disciples, already open to following the God of Israel in repentance, believe and are baptized.

Acts 22:1-21

This is another unusual Gospel presentation because Paul gives it to a hostile crowd that wants to kill him. Nonetheless, we get one more summation from Paul of the Gospel he preaches.

Paul's job is to be a witness of what he has seen and heard (v. 15). Paul is not an actual witness of the resurrection, even though he had seen Jesus on the road to Damascus. He never makes the same claim to be a witness that the other apostles do. In fact, in Acts 13:30-31, when he mentions witnesses of the resurrection, he does not claim to be one of them.

Paul is, however, like the other apostles, appointed by Jesus to be a witness of "what he has seen and heard," if not specifically a witness of the resurrection.

This is almost all that is said about the apostolic Gospel in this passage. As soon as Paul tells them that Jesus appointed him to go to the Gentiles, they shout him down, ending his sermon before he can get any further.

Acts 24:10-21

This is another defense by Paul, this one before the governor Felix. I list it so you can look at it, but I don't find anything relevant to our subject in this dissertation by Paul.

Acts 24:24-25

These two verses are not a Gospel sermon, but Luke does sum up a discussion "concerning the faith in Christ Jesus" by describing it as, "He reasoned about righteousness, self-control, and the judgment to come."

Notice that this discussion about faith in Christ includes "righteousness, self-control, and the judgment." It does not include the atonement. The typical discussion of faith in Christ today includes "man is a sinner," "heaven is a free gift," and "man cannot save himself." Quite a contrast with "righteousness, self-control, and the judgment"!

Acts 26:1-23

We began this booklet with a verse from this sermon by Paul, which is once again a legal defense as well as a Gospel presentation. We will now finish our discussion of the sermons in Acts with this passage because it is the last discussion of the Gospel in the Book of Acts.

Most of the beginning of this defense is simply Paul's story. When he gets to the end, however, he has much to say about what exactly the Gospel is.

Paul tells us that Jesus told him that he would turn the Gentiles "from darkness to light" and "from the power of Satan to God." He said he would do this so that they would receive "remission of sins and an inheritance among those who are sanctified by faith in [Christ]" (v. 18).

These statements imply the importance of repentance in the apostolic Gospel. Clearly, turning from darkness to light and from the power of Satan to God are acts of repentance. However, Paul does not leave us with implications. He makes the clearest statement of the importance of repentance that can be found in Scripture:

> I was not disobedient to the heavenly vision, but declared first to them of Damascus, at Jerusalem, and throughout all the country of Judea, and also to the Gentiles, that they should repent and turn to God, doing works worthy of repentance. (v. 20)

I have to ask again what I asked at the outset of this booklet. Is this the Gospel as it would be summed up by those of us who are descendants of the Reformation?

We all know it is not. There is not a mention of faith here, and Paul says that the call to do good works is part of the Gospel. This is not only different than the Gospel as we Evangelicals typically preach it; by modern standards it is a false Gospel. Do we really want to be found holding a doctrine, and especially a Gospel, that causes us to brand the apostle Paul's Gospel as false?

Paul adds one more description of his Gospel in this passage:

> "I stand to this day testifying both to small and great ... how the Christ must suffer, and how, by the resurrection of the dead, he would be the first to proclaim light to these people and to the Gentiles." (vv. 22-23)

Once again we see the same things that are emphasized in every apostolic Gospel sermon. The emphasis is on the resurrection, which proves that Jesus is the Christ, and an announcement that people should thus respond to him with obedience. Sometimes that obedience is described as repentance, sometimes as faith, once as doing deeds worthy of repentance, and here it is described as light.

Jesus Christ *Is* the Gospel of the Apostles

A dear friend of mine loves to say, "Salvation is not a plan; it's a Man."

We have seen how true this is, at least in the apostles' minds. While Evangelicals almost exclusively preach facts about Christ as the Gospel that must be believed, the apostles preached Christ as a *Person* (a divine Person) that must be believed.

Until we follow in their footsteps, we can be confident that our converts will continue to fall away as quickly and as often as they have been. Charles E. Hacket, the national director of the Division of Home Missions for the Assembly of God, said:

> A soul at the altar does not generate much excitement in some circles because we realize approximately ninety-five out of every hundred will not become integrated into the church. In fact, most of them will not return for a second visit.[11]

How can we expect any other results when we are not preaching the same Gospel that the apostles preached? How can we expect anything better when we are discussing theology with the lost rather than proclaiming the living, resurrected Christ to them?

---

[11] . (cited by Kirk Cameron & Ray Comfort, *The Way of the Master* [Wheaton, IL: Tyndale House Publishers, 2004] p. 61)

Probably the most popular evangelism program in modern history was *Evangelism Explosion,* which was both a program developed by Dr. D. James Kennedy at Coral Ridge Presbyterian Church in the 1960's and a book by the same name published later.

The *Evangelism Explosion* program outlines the Gospel in this way:

1. Eternal life is a free gift; it is not earned or deserved.
2. Man is a sinner and cannot save himself.
3. God is merciful and doesn't want to punish us, but he is just and therefore must punish our sin.
4. Jesus Christ is the infinite God-man. He died on the cross to pay for our sins and rose from the grave to purchase a place in heaven for us.
5. This gift is received by faith. Saving faith is not just head knowledge about God, nor is it just turning to God for temporary needs. It is trusting in Jesus Christ alone for our eternal life.[12]

It is not just *Evangelism Explosion* (EE) that provides this outline. I went through the EE program as a member of an Assembly of God church in 1982. Because the Assembly of God is a Pentecostal denomination, we used an adjusted version of the program called *Evangelism*

---

[12] "Do You Know for Sure"; http://evangelismexplosion.org/resources/online-tracts/english/; accessed March 14, 2013

Challenge, put out by the Pentecostal Church of God. It used exactly the same outline that EE uses.

A few years later, I went through the Southern Baptists' *Continuing Witness Training*. It had an outline of the Gospel that was different, but very similar, emphasizing the same points and "proving" those points with the same Scriptures that the EE program used.

For a couple years, also in the 1980's, I was a member of the Navigator ministries. We were taught to use what they called "the bridge illustration" to present the Gospel. Although "the bridge illustration" was not an outline, it did present the Gospel exactly as *Evangelism Explosion* did, carefully explaining the atonement and emphasizing that we cannot save ourselves without Jesus' sacrifice. The call to believe emphasized belief that Jesus could get us to heaven because of his sacrifice.

Evangelicals[13] would consider themselves to be strict Bible-believers, but almost all of them have missed the Gospel as it was preached by the apostles. Rather than learning from the Gospel proclamations of the apostles, we have taken our careful theological analysis of the apostolic letters and created our own presentation.

As a result, our Gospel proclamation is more a short course on the atonement, faith, and works than it is a proclamation of Christ.

---

[13] As defined in footnote 1

The first Gospels that we are introduced to are the four by Matthew, Mark, Luke, and John. It is clear from statements made in those Gospels that the writers believe that their books are Gospel presentations. Mark, for example, begins his Gospel with:

> The beginning of the Good News of Jesus Christ, the Son of God. (1:1)

Near the end of John's Gospel, John said:

> Jesus did many other signs in the presence of his disciples, which are not written in this book; but these are written, that you may believe that Jesus is the Christ, the Son of God, and that believing, you may have life in his name. (20:30-31)

John, writing a Gospel meant to bring about belief in Jesus Christ, does not ask his hearers to believe what we ask our hearers to believe. He does not ask them to believe that man is a sinner, that heaven is a free gift, that Jesus died for our sins, or that we need to trust him alone to get to heaven. He asks the lost to believe that Jesus is the Christ, the Son of God.

Those who believe that Jesus is the Christ, the Son of God, will be anxious to know what he said. They will be anxious to repent because they know that Jesus will judge them on the last day. They will be anxious to obey because they know that it is Jesus who gives the Spirit, Jesus who forgives sins, and Jesus who is the author of eternal life.

I know that turning us back to the Gospel of the apostles brings up questions about the role of faith and works. This is inevitable. It is our conclusions about the atonement, about faith, and about works that led us to abandon the preaching of the apostolic Gospel so that we could preach a systematic theology concerning the atonement instead.

As a result, returning to the apostolic Gospel is going to bring up the question of *why* the apostles did not preach our atonement theology to the lost.

This is not the place to cover those things. We will do much better at returning to "the faith which was once for all delivered to the saints" (Jude 1:3) if we go one step at a time. The one-step-at-a-time method is less confusing and less frightening.

It is not hard to determine what the apostles preached. As we have seen, their Gospel proclamation was consistent, covering the same points over and over again. Returning to the Gospel as it was proclaimed by the apostles is an excellent first step towards our return to the faith of the apostles.

www.ingramcontent.com/pod-product-compliance
Lightning Source LLC
Chambersburg PA
CBHW072339300426
44109CB00042B/1955